Thank you for finding
this nice little book.

It is said that the longest
journey in life is the journey
from the brain to the heart.

Learning to find your way to the heart
early in life is a great gift.

"I met Gitte Winter Graugaard at a workshop in Nantwich, England, in the fall of 2017. It was a heartwarming meeting with a writer who is passionate about conscious parenthood and balance in the everyday lives of busy families with children. With this book we can help our children find peace within themselves and fill their hearts with love. According to recent research this will affect also the people around them to raise their vibrations as well. Imagine what it will do to the rising children and for generations to come!

Gerd Stautland, Norway
Teacher, mother and grandmother,
Translator of the Norwegian version: I Hjertet Mitt

"My dear friends. This is amaaaazing news – if you love heart connecting and enchanting moments with your child. I love these books, and so do our kids… And now they're in available in multiple languages! Thank you dearest Gitte for your tireless work for more peace and love."

Eva Andrea, Spain
Author and mother
of four children

"The most ingenious thing about this book, I think, is that it also gives the adult a tool – both for conversations with the children, but also for meditations they can do themselves. I recommend that adults read the book twice on their own before reading aloud to a child, so as to become acquainted with the book and its content. The book is perfect for young and old — and I can't wait to introduce it to my children and the people in my life."

Ellen Bucher-Johannessen, Norway
Special needs teacher and
mother of three boys

What parents say about this book:

*"Last night we read The Children's Meditations In My Heart. My oldest
7-year-old son completely calmed down and actually fell asleep at the end
of the story. This morning my younger son of 4 years and I arranged to send
love to our hearts at lunchtime. I love the book."*

*"I got to read the first meditation to my 4-year-old son. He had a hard time
keeping his eyes closed and smiled every time I looked at him. When he
finished I asked, "Now can you sleep well, my most beautiful son?" - "Thank
you, Mom," he replied, and snuggled up smiling."*

*"I use In My Heart for my sensitive daughter who struggles with thought-
rushes at bedtime. They are amazing and do a lot of good for her. I am
divorced from her father, and she uses the exercises when we're not together
and she misses me. In My Heart gets my warmest recommendation."*

*"I love these stories, and so does my daughter... She is barely 6 years old and
has become better at putting her emotions and her love into words. I am
moved by the stories - fantastically written."*

*"It's a great book. I read it almost every night to my 9-year-old son. He asks
me to read it to him."*

*"I have a son who sometimes suffers from anxiety. The meditations are
invaluable when it comes to getting him to drift off to sleep! Even my
14-year-old son sometimes asks me if I can read them to him again."*

*"My son loves this book. He is 10 years old and has ADHD. Highly
recommended."*

To

____

____

____

____

From

____

____

The Children's Meditations
In My Heart

By Gitte Winter Graugaard

Illustrations Elsie Ralston

Room for Reflection Publishing

Thank you Sofie Halkjær for inspiration for heart meditation. To Elsie Ralston for the amazing illustrations. To Katrine Høyer for layout. A big thank you to my lovely children for leading the way into this beautiful universe with such open minds and showing me new paths to heartland.

- Gitte Winter Graugaard

Books in the series The Valley of Hearts are:
- Meet Chief Eaglefeather
- The Flamedancers' Fire
- The Clear Cascade
- The Deep Meadow
- The Mild Winds

Other books published in English:
- Heartlight - teach your child to shine

The series will be available in several languages in the future.
See where we're at with our words here:
www.gittewintergraugaard.dk

The Children's Meditations In My Heart
© Gitte Winter Graugaard 2021
The Children's Meditations In My Heart are protected under Danish copyright law. Copying from this book may only take place at institutions and companies that have entered into an agreement with Copydan within the framework specified in the Agreement.

3rd edition 1st print 2021
Author: Gitte Winter Graugaard
Translation: Maria Laugesen and Kay Xander Mellish
Illustrations: Elsie Ralston
Layout: Katrine Høyer

ISBN: 978-87-93210-65-3 (paperback)
ISBN: 978-87-93210-66-0 (hardbound)
ISBN: 978-87-93210-67-7 (e-book)
ISBN: 978-87-93210-68-4 (PDF)

Room for Reflection Publishing
www.inmyheart.eu
www.gittewintergraugaard.dk

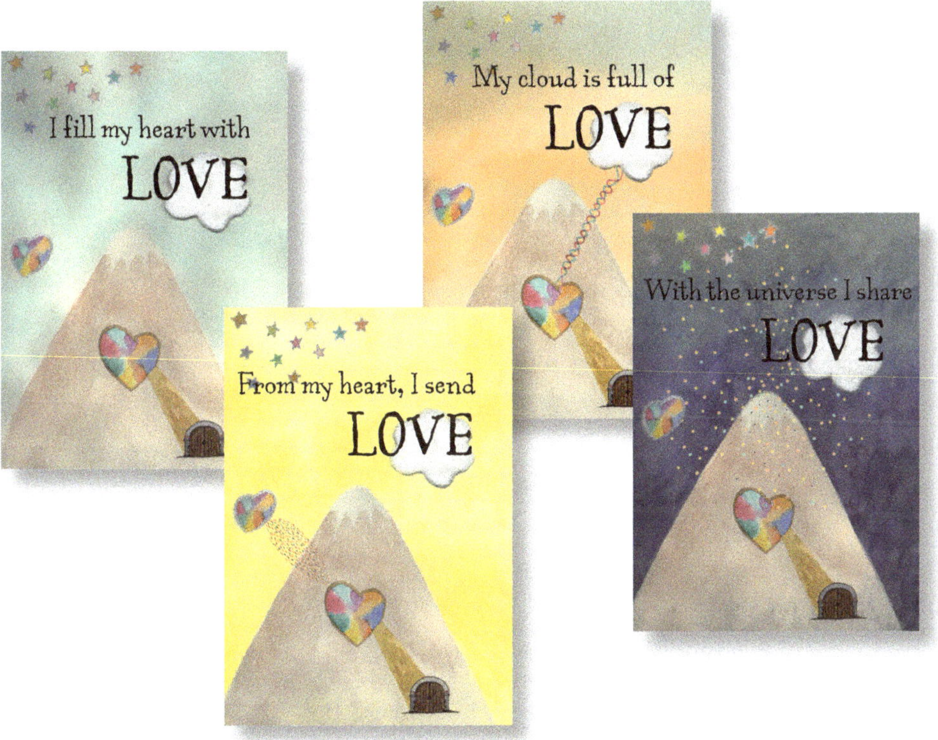

Table of Contents

Introduction

Dear parent,

Congratulations on the loving journey you are about to go upon with your child or children. Thousands of Danish families have already discovered and enjoyed reading these stories and it is such a great pleasure for me to now be able to introduce these meditations all over the world. I feel like a plane of love is about to take off. One by one children will become aware of the beautiful art of self-love all across our beautiful globe.

I am happy to contribute in this BIG small revolution of love. Sadly there are so many things we cannot agree on across borders, however, our love for our children is the same and of most value to any parent. This we can agree on and hence we should focus more upon it.

Children's meditation is lovely for both you and your child. You can read the meditations as bedtime stories. Like many other stories they are all about love. However, by closing their eyes and tuning into their bodies whilst listening to your familiar voice, your child might be able to take in these words of love more fully.

You will now have some loving and calm time together, which is invaluable when our lives are so busy. For a moment, you will come together and turn down the flow of stimuli that constantly surrounds your family.

They say that a modern person gets as much stimulus in one day as our grandparents got in an entire year when they were little. We cannot stop the stimuli around our children, but we can teach them how to navigate a path through digital and societal overload and how to find peace, balance, and most importantly, joy in life.

With "In My Heart" you are teaching your child to go inside themselves to sense their body, mind and heart. Considering the statistics on stress and how it affects our young people, this exercise will be an invaluable lesson for life. By also teaching your child to sense their heart and share their love, you nurture your child's feelings of self-love, harmony and empathy.

Let me establish from the very beginning that I do not doubt for a second that your family love is entirely wonderful and very unique. These meditations are not about the art of loving - you already know that amazing skill.

The Children's Meditations In My Heart and the symbols you get to know from reading the book will help you as a family to:

- Talk about love more

- Become more conscious of your love

- Turn up the love even more

As a parent, you will be doing a guided visualization with your child. Because your child is calmly lying down with closed eyes, your voice can reach even deeper into their beautiful soul.

Many people ask which age groups the meditations can be used for. Heart meditation has no age limit. Children as young as 3 and as old as 18 have told me that they love the stories. Even adults have found that they sleep better after reading these stories.

Heart meditation is not something I came up with. I have merely rewritten the essence of the stories and added elements I myself have been told or encountered in many different meditations. I just love heart meditation and also teach the foundations of these stories to adults through sessions and workshops.

Learn from your child

On this wonderful journey to "Heartland", with your child, please be aware that you can learn a lot from them. Maybe, like many other parents in our generation, you sometimes feel "locked inside your head" but are yearning to feel more in your own heart - to get closer to your "Heartland".

In many ways, children are better at connecting to their hearts than adults. I get a lot of lovely feedback from parents who tell me how impressed they are with how naturally their children approach the stories of "In My Heart", and how easy it is for their children to reach into their hearts.

Children are born in "Heartland" and have a special gift of love to teach us parents. Something special arises between you and your child when you start doing the heart meditations together. I write "together", on purpose, because the room is even more filled with love if you also reach into your own heart and do the exercises at the same time.

Please benefit from this opportunity to leave "Brainland" for a while and meet your child in the wonders of "Heartland". In special moments of heart meditation with your child, you can experience the very fine feeling of unconditional, eternal love that you know from the very first weeks of your child's life, where time for a moment stood absolutely still.

Children want so badly to be where we parents are. If we don't take care, they end up travelling with us to "Brainland". It is so beautiful when we instead leave "Brainland" for a while and meet our children in "Heartland".

Turn up the love

There are many very good recorded children's meditations that your child could listen to. In "In My Heart", the love between you and your child is the focal point, which is why they have not been recorded on audio. Your voice and your presence have a big influence on your child's experience of "In My Heart". The more you turn up the love, the easier it will be for your child to reach into his or her own love as well as yours. Your love comes with a big portion of energy that your child already knows very well and wants to reach into.

Through "In My Heart", you, as a parent, will get a language of the symbols for love. Your love is the same as before, and now you will be able to express yourself in more ways, and expressing our love often leads to relief.

Feel for yourself how many words of love you can accommodate, and how big these words can be, and notice your child's reaction. Play with your words of love and adjust the story to fit your child as much as you feel like. Maybe you already have other symbols for your love. Go ahead and bring them into the meditations. Talk about the symbols you already know and implement them into the story. Maybe your child needs you to talk about a specific emotion or a thought. Adjust the story to fit the situation.

Let your little child invite you into Heartland

When you are both ready, you can turn up the love channel together. Do not be surprised if your child starts using your love words or is ready to turn up the volume before you. Pay attention to your child, enjoy that he or she is so close to his or her "Heartland". Soak up your child's innate wisdom of pure love, wisdom he or she was born with, and embrace it as a gift of life.

When your child lies down safely, closes his or her eyes and listens to your safe, familiar voice, all of your child's channels are open and you have the opportunity to tell your child the most precious stories of love. Through "In My Heart", you can transfer a huge portion of love to your child or children. If your child falls asleep a meditation or whilst you are reading, just keep going. Your child is subconsciously still listening even if he or she is on his way to sleep. Send your child to Dreamland with his or her heart full of love.

My own experience is that "In My Heart" makes children fall asleep faster. If your child has a lot of thoughts and a difficult time letting go of the experiences of the day, "In My Heart" might really help.

When your child removes their focus from all of these thoughts and no longer has to relate to relate to anything else except the pictures that form in their imagination, they experiences a lovely calmness, which makes it easier to fall asleep.

That also means that you can help your child to fall asleep under special circumstances: if your child has a hard time sleeping when you are with friends or family, if you are going for a long ride or flight, if it is noisy around him or her, or if you are on holiday.

This is how you do it:

Before you introduce your child to the meditations, I recommend that you yourself read them once or twice.
You will find some blank spaces along the way
______________________________ , where you can write your child's name.

If you have several children, I recommend that you start with one child at a time. Try to observe whether you are using different words for each of your children. Notice if you have an instinct of what one child needs you to say differs from what another child needs.

Reflect a little about the difference and about what it means to your relationship with each of your children.

If you wish to do the meditations with several children at the same time, you can just say several names and address the children in plural.

On your way you will also meet this sign: ♡ ♡ ♡

The sign is an invitation to make a short pause to give your child room for reflection.

The first few times you read the stories aloud, you might stick completely to the stories. If you wish to change something, just follow your intuition and change words and meanings. Listen to yourself and notice what feels good to you.

Find peace within yourself and find a moment for the meditation when you can feel mindful and calm. Naptime is often a good time for children's meditation, and so is bedtime. The children often fall asleep during your reading, and that is completely fine.

Do not force your child to do the meditation. If you do, it will have no effect. But try to find a way to make your child want to take part.

Have your child lie down in a soft place with a blanket or a duvet. Explain to your child that you want to tell a very special story, full of love. Explain that you are telling this story because you deeply want your child to know how much you love him or her. Just keep on going if your child moves around. The child is still listening.

Sit down comfortably and enjoy a loving, honest and mindful moment with your child. Take some deep breaths yourself before you begin. Feel the calmness descend. Then close your own eyes, breathe deeply and find your way into yourself. Your child will clearly feel your calmness.

Read slowly and take pauses. Let the pictures grow quietly inside your child.

If you experience your children asking about the meditations more often, I very much recommend you to take the time to do them. The ten minutes of intense love that the meditations offer are priceless to both of you. So leave the lunch boxes, work or laundry for later and travel with your child to "Heartland".

You will now find the first of the four meditations. Each of them begins with a special little introduction and each ends with a few encouragements to thought and reflection. I recommend that you do them in chronological order and preferably with some time in between. Through repetition, your child will learn the individual steps, and they will be better preconditioned to continue.

Please, enjoy the wonderful journey you will now embark upon with your child. A precious time is about to begin.

Your own notes

13

This is where the journey
begins.
Let's meditate

The gateway to sleep can
be found within the heart.
In the first meditation,
your child learns to fill
their heart with love and
focus on the strength of
loving themselves.

I fill my heart with LOVE

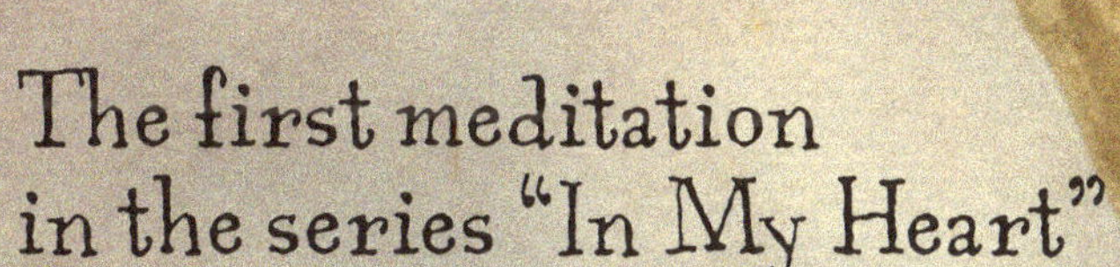

The first meditation
in the series "In My Heart"

Specifically for the children's meditation "I fill my heart with love"

In the first meditation, you guide your child down into the heart and learn to fill it with love. This meditation is the foundation of the other meditations in the series and builds a very special foundation for your child's sense of self-love and self-esteem.

When I started sharing the meditations in this book, it was to teach children to fill their hearts with love. I wanted them to have that gift in life to always know how to find their way into their hearts and learn to fill themselves up with love. Having had a deep contact with my own heart throughout my life has been and is a huge gift. If you have that, you're going to be able to do a lot in life.

Along the way, when my children were little, I learned that the gateway to Dreamland is in the heart. It is much easier for us to fall asleep when we let go of our thoughts and feel the heart instead. Too many children today have trouble sleeping.

Therefore, this meditation and the ones after it can be beneficial for your child's health and well-being if they enable your child to sleep more easily. Sleep has a huge impact on your child's wellbeing and should be taken seriously.

Lend your child your peace and presence and feel for yourself in your own heart along the way. It feels to me like opening a space in front of my body in my heart energy that my child can find peace, love and security in. In that energy, the child's nervous system calms down, and it becomes easy and nice to fall asleep.

But no more writing here because the love mountains are calling for you. Can you hear them? It's your heart whispering to you. It tells you that you and your child are born as light and love.
Have a great time.

I fill my heart with love

Today, we are going on a journey together, you and I. I have really been looking forward to this journey with you. You will come on the journey with me when you listen to my words and create pictures in your own imagination. You do not need to tell me about the pictures. They are yours to keep. But if you want to, we can talk about them later. For now, just listen.

Place your beautiful head on the pillow and close your lovely eyes. Now we'll begin a wonderful journey into your heart – which is full of love.

Breathe calmly, all the way down into your tummy.

♡ ♡ ♡

If you put your hand on your tummy, you might feel it rising and falling with your breath. Just breathe slowly and all the way down into your tummy.

You might feel that you are able to breathe more and more into your tummy for every breath you take.

♡ ♡ ♡

When you want to find peace within yourself, you can ride the back of your breath. Imagine you can float with the air into your body. The slower and deeper your breath, the more calmness you can find.

Now, the story begins. It is a lovely summer day. Imagine you are walking in a beautiful, green meadow with the prettiest flowers in all of your favourite colours. Look, there is a nice flower right there, your very favourite kind. Your flower is so pretty. The grass is wonderfully soft under your bare feet.

The sun warms your body and you feel a nice breeze on your cheek.

Just take some time to look around you while you breathe deeply into your tummy.

Look! Up there, in the tree, there is a little red bird singing. And there is a purple butterfly spreading a loving message in the landscape from flower to flower. Right now it is probably telling everyone that you have arrived. I think it is saying "Look, pretty flower, ___________ (child's name) has come to visit us. Isn't that nice?"

A little bumblebee with pretty stripes and paper-thin wings is buzzing around a bush with beautiful heart-shaped leaves. You pick a leaf and smell it. It smells sweet, like roses.

In front of you, you now see a tall, beautiful mountain. You want to go there. Carefully, you put one foot in front of the other and take a little step on your way. The grass is so pretty and soft under your bare toes. You quickly learn that you can also run, jump and dance in this valley of love – just like you always do.

The mountain is calling for you quietly, and you go closer. You then see a pretty little white fence with a beautiful gate. You want to open it, and when you touch the gate, you can hear it whispering. It is saying: "Welcome, sweet ____________________ . We have been looking forward to seeing you. Go on in. It is such a nice place to be."

Just keep breathing into your tummy. Now we're going a little closer to the mountain.

Behind the little fence you see a trail covered in small, warm, white rocks glittering in the sun. You look around and enjoy all the pretty things you see.

When you walk a little further, you come up close to the mountain. And now you see that there is a big wooden door into the mountain. "The door to ____________________ 's lovely heart", it says on a little sign.

You grab the door, and even though it is big and heavy, you can open it up easily. Because it really wants to open up to you. "Hey there, so good to see you!" the door says to you. You go inside and look around.

Here inside the mountain your lovely heart lives. A heart that has the most profound wishes for you. A heart that whispers to you what to do, when you are in doubt, if you just listen to it. A heart that loves you so incredibly much. A heart, you take with you everywhere you go. A heart so full of love.

Now place your hand on your heart and we will continue. Breathe deeply.

You now see your beautiful heart that lives so neatly inside the mountain. What do you see?
What does your heart look like today?
How has your heart been doing today?
Has it had a good day?
Has it been sad? Has it been angry?
Has it had a good time?
Is your heart small or big today?
What colours does it have?
Is your heart cold or warm today?

If there are other things you want to explore in your heart, do it now.

No matter how your day has been or how your heart is feeling right now, you can always fill it up with love. My love to you is huge. Every single day I send you a lot of love, both when we are together and when we are apart. You can fill your heart with that love, and in the exact same way you can fill up your heart with love yourself. The more love we fill our hearts with the easier our dreams can come true. It is magic.

It is now time to find your 'volume button' in your heart. Can you see a little button right in the middle of your heart? Yes, right there, in the middle of your heart.

Now turn up the button and send love, light, warmth and happiness into your heart. Just turn it up and fill up your lovely heart with love.

Can you find the button? Now you turn it and fill up your heart with love.

Just keep going a little more. And a little more. And just a little bit more. Fill up your heart completely with love.

Feel how the heat from your love is slowly spreading out into your body. Feel how nice it is to fill up your heart with love. Maybe your love has a special colour. Maybe it is spreading out quickly, maybe slowly.

Feel for yourself if your heart could use a little more love and then fill it up even more.

Now let love float from your heart into your body, slowly.

- into your arms
- up into your head. Always remember your head – it is so busy busy busy all day long – it really needs love
- down into your tummy and your back
- down to your legs
- down to your knees
- down to your feet
- and all the way down to your little toe.

Feel for yourself how your beautiful heart can fill up your whole body with love.

You can fill up your body with so much love that it feels like the love reaches further out than your physical body. This is your beautiful heart energy, which is spreading out to all people and animals that are so lucky to be close to you. I am so lucky to be close to you right now.

The power of love in your heart is like the wildest magic. With that power you can turn tears into smiles, make dark clouds disappear and warm up cold hearts. You truly are a superhero with love power. Take good care of your magical power of love.

My love for you is everlasting. Now feel for yourself how much love you also hold within yourself. Feel how nice it is to fill up your own heart with love. Love from other people is wonderful. However, the love you hold in your heart is your amazing superpower.

Ending – pick the one that fits your situation

Daytime: Now you are slowly getting ready to come back to this room. When you are ready, you will open up your eyes and you will wake up with a heart full of love.

Bedtime: Now you are ready to sleep. You can now safely travel to Dreamland with your heart full of love. Sleep well, my lovely child.

Reflections after the meditation
"I fill my heart with love"

If your child is sleeping, you can choose to stay close to him or her a little longer.

Notice how you are feeling right now. Listen to all the thoughts running through your mind. Feel your emotions in your body.

Maybe you have filled your heart with love together with your child. Maybe you now want to fill up your heart with love. Maybe your heart also needs a refill after all the tasks of today. Maybe you also need to leave your "Brainland" for a while and visit your "Heartland".

Walk quietly through the meadow and into your mountain, and fill up your heart with love. Spend some time to try to feel for yourself if you fill up your heart with love often enough. Many parents forget themselves and tend only to fill up everybody else with love.

Repeat the meditations after a few days with your child, when you are calm. Notice if your child already has a different attitude towards the meditation. Maybe your child will ask you if you will please read the stories about the heart again. In the time to come, try to notice if you get a feeling of having opened an extra channel of love between you and your child. How does it feel to say all those loving words to your child? How does your child react to your loving words?

For some parents, it can feel very liberating to verbalize their great love for their children. For others, it can be intimidating. This is closely related to which words you heard yourself when you were growing up. Despite your own upbringing, you can now choose for yourself which words you want to send through your love channel to your child. And maybe those same words will be repeated when your child someday opens a love channel to his or her child.

In our house, we have made a little song that we sing occasionally. It is sung in a simple, little random melody by just repeating:

"I fill my heart with love

I fill my heart with love

I fill my heart with love

I fill my heart with love."

We sing it when we feel that one of us needs love. It can be on the way to school, in kindergarten, after an argument or when someone is upset. And because our children have been doing this meditation on a regular basis for several years (since they were 3 and 6), they know exactly what to do when they hear the song. In that way, they can touch base with the meditations at any time.

Your own notes

28

When we know the way
to our heart, we can meet
there in our great love
for each other.

From my heart, I send
LOVE

The second meditation
in the series "In My Heart"

Specifically for the children's meditation "From my heart, I send love"

In the first meditation "I fill my heart with love", you taught your child to fill his or her heart with love. In this meditation, you will teach your child to send and receive love to and from others.

By talking about how we send and receive love over distance, your child will get an extra feeling of being loved, even when you are not together – either because of your busy schedules or during periods of being physically separate.

For this meditation, I recommend that you first lie down with your child on the bed or for instance on a couch. Lie down on your sides, facing each other.

From my heart, I send love

Today, we will focus on how we send and receive love. We can send love to the people we love, even when we cannot be together. And in the same way, we can receive love from the people we miss from a distance and let it float right into our hearts.

Now close your lovely eyes and breathe deeply into your tummy. Spend some time feeling yourself getting calmer and calmer.

Breathe. Just breathe. Long low breaths are so important for us to become calm.

Ride the back of your breaths all the way into your beautiful heart. Keep going a little more. Deep, long breaths.

♡ ♡ ♡

Try to see if you can send the air deeper into your tummy each time you breathe. Keep going a little more.

♡ ♡ ♡

You are now in front of the little, pretty, white fence on the meadow again. The fence you know from when we learned how to fill our hearts with love. Take some time to imagine all of it again. See the colours come alive in the meadow.

It is summer and it is nice and warm. Your bare toes are in the grass. Now you see your mountain in the distance, and you know that your beautiful heart lives inside that awesome mountain.

You begin to walk towards the mountain.

You have now reached the mountain. You quickly find the door that says: "The door to _____________________ 's lovely heart".

As always, the door opens up easily. Because it really wants to open up to you. "Hi there," the door says to you, when you go inside and look around. "Welcome back to your heart, sweet _____________________."

Your lovely heart lives inside this mountain. A heart that wants all the best in this world for you. A heart that whispers to you what to do, when you are in doubt, if you just listen to it.

Now place your hand on your heart.

You now know what we are going to do. We are going to ask how your heart is feeling, and then we are going to fill it up with love.

So take a look at your heart. What do you see? What does your heart look like today?

- How does it feel?
- How is your heart doing today?
- Has it had a good day?
- Has it been sad? Has it been angry?
- Has it had a good time?
- Is it small or big today?
- What colours does it have?
- Is it cold or warm?

If there are other things, you want to examine in your heart, do it now.

No matter how your heart is feeling right now, what it looks like, and how your day has been, we are now going to fill your beautiful heart up with love. In this way you can end every day with a heart full of love, which will automatically make you wake up in the morning full of the most beautiful and powerful heart energy. So find that little button in your heart, turn it up and fill your heart with love.

Just keep going a little more. Fill up your big, beautiful heart with love.

Fill up your heart with love, just keep going.

Feel how nice it is. Feel the love running from your heart and into your beautiful body. It is like an inner shower of love.

♡ ♡ ♡

Right now, I am doing the same thing from my heart. Right now, I am also filling up my own heart with love, and in a minute, we will try to send love to each other. Actually, we do it all the time without even thinking about it, but the difference now is that we will pay close attention to what happens when we send love to each other. By observing the way we send and receive love, we can turn it up when we need to.

Now let's each take one of our hands and move them from our own heart to each other's heart. And then we'll lie here and notice how it feels.

What can you feel? What is happening inside of you, when you are feeling my heart? Can you already feel all the love I have for you? Can you feel how much I love you? My love for you is so enormous. From the very first time I saw you, I have loved you with all of my heart.

Now I begin to imagine that I am sending a lot of love into your heart. I am sending love from my heart, into my arm, into my hand and into your heart.

Try to feel for yourself if you can feel my great love for you. It lives in my heart and is now flowing directly from my heart to yours, because I love you very much.

I am now sending my love to you. Can you feel my big love for you?

I now send you my greatest love, filled with light, warmth and joy to make you feel how much I love you. Keep lying down a little longer and feel how nice it is to be loved in the way you are. And I feel how amazing it is to get to love you.

I feel extremely thankful that precisely YOU are my child. That you and I are family.

Now, I am going to turn up my love a little more. Try to feel me turning it up. Can you feel it?

Now it is your turn to try to send some love. Love works in many ways. We can fill our own hearts with love, we can receive love from others, and we can also get more love from loving others. When we love others very much, our hearts automatically become full with even more love. The more we turn up the love in our hearts, the more we can also love others.

When you are ready, you will close your eyes and focus on your beautiful heart that you just filled up with love.

Find the little button in your heart again. When you have found it, imagine yourself sending a wave, a flow, a ray of love out through your arm and your hand and right into my heart.

Your hands are incredible channels for your superpower of love.

It can feel like love, light, warmth or joy. The way we do it is different from person to person, so try to find your own way of doing it. I already know you can, because I often feel the great love you are giving to me.

It feels good when you send your love to me. It is as if I can feel that very special, magical power of love you keep inside of you.

Now try to see if you can turn up or down your flow, ray or wave. Then you can decide for yourself how much you want to send. Keep going a little more, until you can feel that you have sent out a nice portion of love.

And then slowly turn down the ray, wave or flow and go back into yourself. Take the power of love home to yourself.

♡ ♡ ♡

Thank you so much for this great love you have sent to me. It means the world to me to lie down close to you and feel your love. I feel so blessed, thankful and loved right now. Thank you.

♡ ♡ ♡

Now let's try to send love to someone who isn't here right now. Try spreading out your hands to the side so the insides are pointing out. Then imagine that you have two powerful love channels in your hands. Like the wildest fairytale character or a cool superhero, you can send out your power of love through your hands. Imagine how far out into the world it reaches. Your power of love is huge and such a strong source.

Now try sending out your love through your hands. Think of someone out there you would like to reach with your power of love.

It could be someone you care about or someone you miss. Picture him or her in your mind – and watch him or her receive your love in their heart.

Try turning up your power of love and try turning it down.

Brilliant! You are so good at loving. I bet the one you are thinking about pauses right now wherever he or she is and smiles. And with every smile you generate in this world you make the world a better place to live.

Before we finish, we should make sure that your own heart is still filled up. So you will now finish by filling your heart with a little more love to yourself. Find the button and fill yourself up with love.

Sometimes we give everything we have to others and we forget ourselves. We always need to remember to love ourselves deeply. And then there will automatically be more magical power of love in our hearts.

When you have filled up your own heart again, you can lie down and think about all the great love you have just sent to me and feel the love I have sent to you. How incredibly fortunate we are to be parent and child. From all the children in the whole wide world – I feel so blessed to lie here with you and have the privilege to be your parent. I love you very much.

In this way, we can always send love to each other. We don't even need to lie down together and hold each other's hands. Because the power of love is filled with an energy that can reach around the whole world. So no matter how far apart we are, we can always send and receive love to and from each other.

Ending – choose the one that fits

Daytime: Now it is time to come back to the room. When you are ready, you will open up your beautiful eyes and wake up with a heart full of love.

Bedtime: Now you are ready to sleep with your lovely heart full of love. Sleep well.

Reflections after the meditation
"From my heart, I send love"

Notice how you are feeling right now. Listen to all of your thoughts as they emerge. If your child is asleep, you can rest a little longer. Maybe you now feel like filling up your own heart with love. Maybe you want to send love to someone you care about or someone you miss. Go quietly through the meadow, into your mountain, fill up your heart with love, and start sending love to the one you have in mind.

Repeat the meditation in a few days with your child. Once you are comfortable with the exercise, you can try to do it without holding your hands on each other's hearts. Lie down with more and more distance in between you and practice sending love over longer and longer distances.

For example, if my husband is on a trip, I send him love together with my children. When the three of us send him love at the same time and hold hands, our love can fly all the way to Asia, where he often travels, and we can feel him stepping up to receive our love in his heart wherever he is. That gives the children a feeling of contact with their father even though he is very far away.

Try to also put your hand on your child's heart in other situations and come up with a mutual signal that you are now sending love. It can be when your child is going to bed, after a conflict, or when you are going to be apart from each other for a little while. Create a little love signal to use with each other.

In our house, we signal that we are sending love to each other by putting our hand on our own hearts and then turning it around to the other person.

If I say goodbye to my children at school, when they are standing behind a window amongst or other kids or teachers, we have our own little silent signal to tell each other that we are thinking about each other and sending love.

As a parent, we send many loving thoughts to our children throughout the day. Remind your child that you are sending him or her love, even when you are not together physically. And remind your child that he or she can always send love from his or her heart to you or someone he or she misses or cares about. In that way, you are opening up your channel of love, even when you are not together.

You can also try to arrange a specific time to send each other love. If you know that your child is doing something special during the day that might be difficult, you can tell her that you will send love and help at precisely the moment the challenge is taking place. If my oldest daughter is upset at school, she puts her hand on her heart and extracts some of that love she knows that I am sending her, and finds comfort.

We will work more on retrieving love in the third meditation in this series, "My cloud is full of love".

Variations
When you have become familiar with sending love to each other, you can try sending love to others as well. Here are some examples:

Siblings: Sending love to each other is powerful and heartwarming for siblings. Ask them to lay down facing each other and do the exercise together. Teach them that they belong together and have an eternal love for each other.

Tell them that the love between siblings is so strong that they can share it for the rest of their lives, whether they are together or apart. Do the exercise when the children are playing well together, and then try it another time when they have had a conflict. Observe what happens between the children after the meditation.

Notice if their relationship to each other changes when they send each other love. If you are going on a vacation together and do the exercise on a daily basis, you can create a very special chemistry between your children during the vacation.

Family and friends: Your child can also share love with family and friends that he does not see very often and misses. Perhaps one parent travels a lot, or the parents live apart from each other. Your child can also share love with a grandparent or a good family friend who isn't nearby.

Ask your child to think about the person he misses and cares about. Start by asking your child to imagine what that person looks like. Then ask your child to fill his heart with love and send love in a wind, wave or ray to the person who isn't present.

Let your child enjoy the feeling of sharing this love with the person he cares about, whether they are close to each other or far apart.

You could explain this exercise to the person your child is thinking of, and let that person send love back to your child. It will be nice for your child to be able to talk to, for example, a grandmother about sending love to each other when they are apart. It would be nice to share the meditations with this person who is physically distant, opening up a channel for even more love to enter your child's life.

Other examples for good use of this meditation is – soldier families, parents in prison, sick parents in hospitals etc.

In conflict: We can also send love to someone we are in conflict with, to try to open up for understanding, kindness, and forgiveness in our hearts. It is not easy, but it has a big effect. When we send love to someone we are in a conflict with, we can't help but change our view of the person. We see that person in a warmer light, and we might find new paths towards reconciliation.

Children often find this exercise easier, because their irritation usually is not as deep as the anger of an adult. This makes meditation a very useful conflict tool for children.

Try it for yourself as well. It can truly build bridges. After all, we are all humans – and if we can agree on anything it would be that we all long for love.

When you have become comfortable with this meditation, please continue to the meditation, "My cloud is full of love", which teaches your child to retrieve the love you send her in her cloud of love.

Your own notes

46

When we learn
that love is an energy
that can travel over
distance, we can get a hug
from someone we miss.

My cloud is full of LOVE

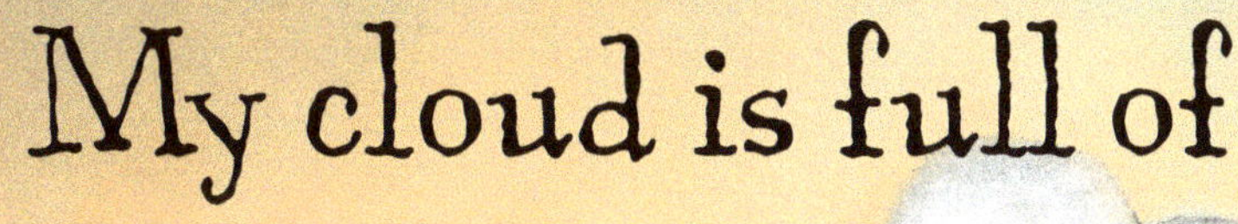

The third meditation
in the series "In My Heart"

Specifically for the children's meditation "My cloud is full of love"

Imagine the pleasure in your child's heart if he or she knew how often you think about him/her during your day. With this third heart meditation, you'll get the opportunity to express how often you think about your child and how much love you send to your child with those thoughts every single day.

A love that your child can pick up in the cloud and fill into his/her heart when needed.

My cloud is full of love

This meditation is special for me to share with you, because it will show you how much I think about you every day. I think about you when we are together, but I also think about you when we are apart.

If you knew how often I think about how wonderful you are and how much I love you when we are away from each other, you would be happy in your heart. When you know how often I think about you, when we are not together, you will feel that I am closer to you than you sometimes think I am.

Today we are going to take a closer look at a little cloud in the sky that always floats above you. In that cloud, my love for you lives, and if you get to know the cloud, you will know that I am always there with you, no matter how far apart we are. In fact, the cloud is full of love from ALL the people who care about you and hold you in their hearts.

The cloud is very cool and it already knows your name, because it is a very good friend. It has always been your friend and it has always been there, and today you are going to get to know it very well.

So close your eyes and breathe deeply into your tummy. Try to see if you can lie still.

♡ ♡ ♡

Breathe slowly. Try to see if you can breathe more deeply into your tummy each time you breathe in.

Feel your tummy rising and falling. Rising and falling. Feel your body relaxing.

♡ ♡ ♡

Try to see if you can breathe in through your nose and out through your mouth.

♡ ♡ ♡

We are now lying here very still, finding our way into our own peace, and just looking forward to meeting the cloud.

♡ ♡ ♡

Breathe deeply a little longer.

♡ ♡ ♡

Imagine you are standing in that beautiful, green meadow in front of your mountain. You can see the mountain right in front of you. The big wooden door is open, and behind the door you can see you heart. Your big, lovely, beautiful heart. Just go on in, and see how your heart is feeling today.

♡ ♡ ♡

When you have checked in on your heart, you begin to fill it up with love just like you have done before. It is always nice to visit your heart and fill it up with love.

Find the button and turn up your magical power of love.

Now imagine that you are seeing a nice, colourful thread from your heart going out through a little hole high up in your mountain.

Through the little hole, you can spot a little cloud waving at you. Walk out of the door again and look up to that little hole in the mountain, where the thread is coming out. The thread is as pretty outside as it is inside your mountain. In fact, it is even more colourful outside the mountain, where the sun is shining on it so beautifully. It carries all the colours of your heart, and it sparkles in the light. It is so pretty. Wow, take a look at it. So beautiful.

Try now to follow the thread with your eyes and watch how it is attached to the prettiest little cloud on the sky. Your cloud. Your cute, beautiful cloud of love.

♡ ♡ ♡

Listen! It is speaking to you. "Hi, _________________ ," the cloud says to you. It has a loving voice, because it is full of love.

"I have been looking forward to you noticing me so much. If you miss someone you love or if you are feeling lonely, you can always pull me closer to you like a balloon on a string. I am always ready to come with hugs and kisses from all the people you love and who love you."

This pretty cloud is full of all the love that I and everyone else who loves you deeply sends to you every day through our loving thoughts and with our heart energy that flows freely. Your cloud is full of the purest and finest love.

Many times during the day, when I cannot be with you, I think of you, and I miss you and look forward to seeing you again. I think about what you might be doing, and how you are doing. As I think about you, I am sending you a stream of love. Imagine now that all these loving thoughts are flowing from my heart up into your cloud, which is connected to your heart.

From the cloud, you can pick up a nice ray of love as often as you want. Like the finest, shiniest ray of thoughts full of love and gratitude for being your parent. I am so happy that you – precisely you – have become my child.

Now look up and see your little cloud floating above you everywhere you go. Imagine that you are at school or at kindergarten sitting on a chair, or maybe playing in the yard, or in the playground. Imagine that you look up from whatever you are doing and see your thread floating in the air up to your little cloud.

Now imagine that you are grabbing the thread and pulling the cloud closer – so close that it can come all the way down to you and hug you. Your cloud is full of hugs and love from all of us who love you. There is so much love in that cloud. We keep filling it up so you can never empty it out.

Try to feel those nice, warm hugs and all of the beautiful love your cloud contains. Notice how you become wrapped in the cloud's warm hug. The cloud tells you that love travels with you everywhere you go, because you are so loved.

Now pull the cloud closer to you and let go again.

Closer and further away. Closer and further away.

You decide how close to you, you want to keep the cloud, or how close to you it needs to be. Where you want the cloud to be can easily change from day to day. Some days it is nice to have it hanging right over your shoulder, while on other days you might want to send it all the way up to the sky.

Imagine again the playground where you are playing. Can you see all the children running around? Try looking up into the sky. Can you see that each of the kids has his own or her own special cloud of love?

All children have a cloud of love. But not all parents have told their children about the cloud yet.

Whether or not all children know about their cloud, it is hanging right over their heads.

Look around in the playground again and notice that some of your teachers and school staff also have clouds of love above their heads. Some adults know about their clouds, and some don't.

Maybe their parents haven't told them about their clouds yet. So you are so lucky to get to know your cloud as a child. And I am so happy to tell you about your special cloud.

Our clouds are with us everywhere we go, no matter how old we are. Right now, my cloud is also with me, and it is hanging above my head. Maybe you can see mine too? All the people who love me help fill my cloud with love. So when you think of me during the day and send me a loving thought, it ends right here in my beautiful cloud. And for that I thank you and feel very blessed.

Now keep your eyes closed and notice the room we are in right now. Your cloud might be right here in the room. Or it might be in the dark sky outside. Imagine looking through your window into the dark sky outside the house right now, and feeling the cloud up there.

Hear the cloud calling for you.

"Hi, _______________________ . Here I am. I am so happy that you know me now. I have been up here all the time, but now that you know me, it is easier for me to help you when you are sad or need a hug.

I would very much like to give you all the hugs and loving thoughts from your mum and dad and all the people who love you. All their loving thoughts are right here inside of me waiting for you. So just pull your thread, sweet _______________________ , and I will come down to you and give you a hug. A hug full of love, light, warmth, joy and safety from your mum and dad. Remember that I am always with you, no matter where you go."

"Come, let us fill up your heart with love together. Just fill it up when

you are ready and I will help sending love from your loved ones on to you. Are you ready? Here we go. Just keep filling it up. Maybe you can fit in a little bit more. There we go - keep going! A little bit more."

Ending – choose the one that fits.

Daytime: Now you are ready to come back to this room. Slowly open up your eyes and wake up with a heart full of love.

Nap or nighttime: Now you are ready to sleep with your lovely heart full of love. Sleep well, my beautiful child. I love you very much.

Reflections after the meditation
"My cloud is full of love"

If your child has fallen asleep, you can keep lying there a little longer and reflect about your own reactions to the meditation. Maybe you want to think about your own cloud for a little bit. Notice how you are feeling right now. Can you sense your own cloud of love?

You too have a cloud. Try thinking back to your own childhood. Did you have a feeling of having a cloud or something similar? Did your parents use similar symbols? How was your feeling of being connected to your parents when you were a child? How is your feeling of being connected to them today?

Who else is filling love into your cloud? Think about all the people you have around you who think of you and send you loving thoughts that end up in your cloud.

Who is filling up your cloud with love? If your parents are still alive, they are also thinking about you every day and filling love into your cloud - even in their own funny ways. If they are no longer alive, you can think of all the love they have already put into your cloud and know that even old love can live in the cloud and will never run out.

Depending on your beliefs, you might think that they are still filling love into your cloud from where they are today. To me that thought is so beautiful.

Your partner or a good friend can of course also fill up your cloud with love. How is your feeling of being connected with your partner or a good friend today? And remember that your children also send you much love during the day, which also ends up in your cloud. Maybe more love than you can imagine.

Also notice how many wonderful clouds your loving thoughts contribute to filling up every single day.

In the time to come you can try talking about the little cloud with your child. You can ask your child about the cloud, reminding him or her of the cloud and describing the thoughts you are sending your child. Give examples of your thoughts sometimes to make the thoughts become more concrete for your child.

Children in sorrow – a hug from the sky

Accordingly to your belief, the little cloud can be a nice symbol of love for your child if you are going to say goodbye to someone you love. Clouds can, as I mentioned before, float all the way up into the sky.

When we love with all of our hearts, and have to say goodbye, the big words often come to us naturally. Just writing those words makes my stomach curl up and my throat tighten – because saying goodbye to the people we love the most is painful. For children the pain is also unbearable.

If your child is saying goodbye to someone he is very close to, the two of them can agree that your child can send his or her cloud of love up into the sky and still let the person, who soon (or already) belongs in the sky, fill up the cloud with love. A love your child can retrieve when he or she misses them, by pulling the cloud close and getting a hug from the sky or heaven if you like.

Fill it up from Paris

In our home, we often talk about our clouds. My oldest daughter (who was then 7) asked me one day: "When I have taken all the love from my cloud that I need, can I give what is left to other children in my class, who also need love?" Of course, she can do that. However, we also had a good talk about how all children have a cloud, that most parents love their children very much and send lots of love to their children during their workday, but that some parents just have not told them about the cloud yet.

A few weeks later, I was travelling to Paris, and my youngest daughter (who was then 5) was sad when I dropped her off at kindergarten. I asked her if she could see her cloud, and where it was. She pointed at her shoulder and said: "It is right here, Mummy, because I need to keep it very close to me today. Because I miss you already."

At night, when I was putting her to bed and saying goodbye, she was in a good mood, and I asked her where the cloud was now. "All the way up amongst the stars, Mummy. Because that way it is easier for you to find it, when you are in Paris. And then you can fill it up with love, even though you are far away." So she has a feeling of being able to pull the "thread" and pull the cloud close, when she misses me.

Love is exactly the same – the nice thing about the meditations is that the children get a language of love, and that we can talk about the love, which is already there and growing between us.

Your own notes

62

Once we understand that
love is an energy that can
travel in time and space, we
can also send it
into the Universe and
learn to meet the world
with an open heart.

With the universe I share

LOVE

The fourth meditation
in the series "In My Heart"

Specifically for the children's meditation "With the universe, I share love"

In this fourth meditation, your child will learn how to share his or her love with the universe and with children who do not experience the same kind of love you are so lucky to have in your family.

The meditation has three general purposes. The first one is training your child's ability to feel empathy and gratefulness. The second one is creating a feeling of being able to make a difference in the world by opening up one's heart. The third purpose is creating a feeling of connectedness with the universe in your child.

When we begin working with the feeling of belonging together in the universe and sense that we can affect each other's lives through love, we create a wonderful feeling of cohesion and unity, which is much nicer than the individualistic and somewhat tough, performance-focused approach that many people in our generation grew up with.

Every parent has his or her own thoughts about what children need to know about what is going on in the world. In this meditation, I will talk about lonely children, and I will touch upon war and hunger. You can choose to add more or fewer details according to your child's age and your own beliefs about what you want your child to know about the children of the world.

With the universe, I share love

Today we are sending our love all the way up to the stars. Yes, to think that your love can float all the way up to the stars. Maybe you too have looked up into the stars and thought: "There are so many stars, and they are so beautiful."

Today, we are playing with the love magic of the stars, and you will find that your own love is magical as well. You truly are a superhero with a special power of love.

When you look up into the sky full of stars, it is so far away that other children around the world can see the same stars as you. Children in the whole world look up at the stars. All over the world, children and adults love the stars, and many people think to themselves that the stars are magical. When we see a shooting star, a wish may come true.

There is a nice little poem, which goes like this:

> Star light, star bright,
> The first star I see tonight
> I wish I may, I wish I might
> Have the wish I wish tonight.

Stars mean many things to us, and we attach many emotions to stars. When someone dies, we sometimes say that they have become a beautiful shining star in the sky. A few clever scientists even think that we are made from no less than stardust. In that way, we can say that we are stars ourselves that can shine. Our inner light shines when we listen to our hearts and trust that the voice of our heart is true. Imagine if you light your inner light in your heart with your love and a star is watching down on you thinking "What a beautiful, loving child full of light."

Just like that, you are also a shining star in the night. You should know that you can always go into your heart and turn up your light with your great love.

Now start by closing your lovely eyes and lie down comfortably.

Just close your beautiful eyes now, and feel the peace spreading out into your body.

♡ ♡ ♡

Feel your strong muscles beginning to relax. Notice the sounds around you and let them just float on, while you focus on your breathing.

♡ ♡ ♡

Breathe deeply into your tummy. Keep breathing in more and more air. Breathe in through your nose and out through your mouth. Each time, try to breathe even further into your tummy.

Keep going a little longer. Put your hand on the bottom of your tummy and feel it moving up and down when air comes into and out of your tummy.

Now, go into your heart. Look and feel how your heart is doing today. How has the day been for your lovely heart?

Has your heart had a good day or a bad day? A fun day? Or a crazy day? A quiet day or a busy day? Maybe you can see some colours in your heart. Maybe you can see if your heart is big or small today. No matter what kind of day your heart has had, you can always fill it up with love before going to bed.

Your heart loves it when you come to visit, when you let go of the thoughts in your head for a little while and you move your attention to your body to check on your heart.

Just fill more love into your heart and feel how nice it feels when the magical power of love spreads out into your body. Feel how wonderful it can be to visit your heart and turn off your thoughts for a while. Thoughts are good, but they can be very noisy in our heads. So just enjoy that you can turn them off for a while, and enjoy being right here right now in your great, beautiful heart.

Now notice all the loving elements we know so well from the heart meditations. Imagine that you are standing in front of your beautiful mountain, looking at it. Notice the big wooden door leading into your beautiful heart. See that our hearts are sending love to each other. Find the little, pretty cloud of love hanging above the mountain, connected with your heart by the little thread going into the mountain.

All these elements are full of love and are part of our family. They describe, in so many ways, the great love we have between us. A love I am very thankful for sharing with you. I love you so incredibly much. I am very happy that precisely you are my child, and that the two of us could be part of the same family.

Luckily, there are many families with lots of love. But unfortunately, not all children grow up with the kind of love that we share. Not all children grow up with their parents. Some children don't even have a home. Some don't have a bed, and they have to sleep wherever they can find a place, sometimes right on the street.

Many children feel all alone in the world. Some children's parents have died, other parents are sick and others again have been forced away from their children, for example because of war or hunger. We have every reason to be very grateful for the love we share in our family. It is nice to feel grateful and to understand how fortunate we are.

Here comes the magical part. With a little help from the stars, we can actually share our love with the children who need love in their lives. We can share our great love and feel connected to children of the whole world. Let me tell you how.

♡ ♡ ♡

You have just filled up your heart with love. That is important, because when we love ourselves and fill ourselves up with love, it is also easier for us to help others. Just as we can send love to each other, you can now send love out into the universe with your magical superpower of love.

So imagine now that you are sending out love through the magical channels of love in your hands and up through the roof. You can also let love fly out the window or float up through a chimney. Find the way that suits you best. Now, see your love leaving the house in a wave or a ray, and follow it all the way up to the stars. Float on the back of your love all the way up into the stars. Maybe it is a little further away. Maybe you are already there.

When you make it all the way up to the stars, imagine that your love is the finest, prettiest magic dust. Maybe it is golden, or maybe it has colours. Only you know. Now imagine that you are floating around with your love from star to star and quietly sprinkling your love onto the stars. Watch it as it lands so neatly right on top of the stars. Maybe you have love for many stars; maybe you want to sprinkle all of your love onto a few stars or maybe just one star – you decide how you feel. Keep going a little more.

Now look at your magic love dust lying there, shining like the prettiest, clearest starlight. Now ___________________ 's love is lying so neatly and beautifully on top of these pretty stars.

Just keep going a little longer, and enjoy seeing your love sparkle on the stars in the night.

Now imagine a lonely child somewhere on earth. A child who is looking up at the stars right now and asking for more love in their life. Imagine what that child looks like, and feel how you think that child is feeling. No child likes to feel lonely. All children want to love and be loved.

And look what happens now! Now your love dust is raining down over that child and filling up that child's heart with love. Right now, that child is feeling your love. Right now, you are filling up the universe with love. And right now, that child knows that somewhere on earth, there is a friend who is ready to share his or her love.

That friend is you, and right now, your love is spreading out into the universe and reaching into a lonely child's heart. Feel for yourself how that feels inside of you. Feel how nice it is to spread love to the people who need it the most.

Feel how spreading love is also very nice for you. We can all spread our love to those lonely children and adults living with us here on Earth and looking up at the same stars in the night. The stars connect us and give us the courage to believe and hope.

Ending – choose the one that fits

Daytime: You are now ready to come back into the room or the living room. Slowly, you will open up your eyes and wake up with your heart full of love. You will know that your love is spreading out into the universe.

Nap or nighttime: You are now ready to sleep with your heart full of love, knowing that your love is spreading out into the universe. Sleep well, my little darling.

Reflections after the meditation
"With the universe, I share my love"

Notice how this meditation makes you feel. What does it mean to you to see your child spreading his or her love to the universe? What thoughts does it bring to mind about your own love? About your own connectedness to the universe and to the lonely people on the earth?

If you feel like it, do the same exercise for yourself. Fly up to the stars and spread out your love like the finest magic dust over the stars. Notice who is right now asking for your love, and how it feels to know that your love can be shared with other people, who might be far away, through the stars.

Maybe you will find through the meditation that the feeling of increased connectedness is also nice for you. When we live in an individualistic culture, tapping into this feeling of connectedness can be incredibly pleasant.

Maybe, in the time after the meditation, you will want to send love to strangers on your way. It can be the homeless, the busy, the errant, the sick, the dying – or someone you know. Your love can spread through a loving look, a helping hand, a pat on the back. Your love can reach incredibly far, just by you paying a little more attention to it. And by paying more attention to the limitations your love has, and where those limiting beliefs come from.

These meditations to the universe are incredibly powerful and have a good effect on our hormone production. Notice what is happening in your body. Notice what is happening in your heart. Notice how you are feeling right now.

You now know all four meditations in the series "In My Heart". Mix them freely as you like, and use them in a way that fits into your family's life.

Let us together fill up homes all over the world with the most beautiful heart energy created by love to and from our children. Can life get any bigger than that?

Your own notes

76

Which meditation do you
like the most?

Conversation after meditation

We can learn a lot about love if we listen to our children's experiences of meditation. Here are some questions to help you get started. Come up with more for yourself.

Which meditation is your favourite?

    1. I fill my heart with love (green)

    2. From my heart, I send love (yellow)

    3. My cloud is full of love (orange)

    4. With the universe I share love (purple)

Why do you like it best?

____

____

____

____

____

How does that meditation feel inside you?

Did you see it as a little movie? If so - what did you see?

The gateway to Dreamland is hiding in our hearts. Many children sleep better with meditation. Have the meditations also made you sleep easier, better or faster?

How did you feel when you woke up the next day?

Do you remember what you dreamt after meditation?

82

____

____

____

____

____

____

____

____

____

____

____

Do you remember what you dreamt after meditation?

Tips for remembering your dreams: Say out loud before you sleep that you wish to remember your dreams. When you wake up in the morning ask yourself as the first thing you do, what you have dreamt. (We can learn a lot from our dreams.)

Do you like to draw?

What does your
Love Mountain
look like?

What does your
heart look like?

If you remember what you dreamt, you can draw it here :

If you could see images during your heart meditation, draw one of them here:

Draw your Heart or Love Mountain here with all the colours and details you've seen or felt:

About the Author

The *Children's Meditations In My Heart* has been written by Gitte Winter Graugaard (b. 1977). Gitte is passionate about writing books to strengthen the imaginations of children, as well as nurture their intuition and help them create balance in life. Heart meditation in a mountain is an old tradition across many cultures and religions.

Gitte holds a Masters Degree in Business Administration and has worked in Communication, specialising in storytelling. She is also a trained Life Mastery Coach, Heartcore Mentor, Mindfulness Instructor and Conscious Transformer. In 2019 Gitte gave a passioned TEDx speech in England about helping children to sleep by being present as a parent. We recommend that you to watch it here: www.gittewintergraugaard.dk/tedx

However, her most important knowledge about the beautiful art of listening to her heart, comes from Gitte's own life, which is filled with love and heart choice. Now you know all four meditations and can mix them freely as you wish, to fit into your family's everyday life.

On the pages after each meditation, you can write small notes about your own and your child's comments on their heart meditation experiences. We also recommend that you encourage your child to draw their version of the mountain, heart, cloud or any of the other symbols. Children's drawings often provide a great opportunity for a good conversation.

Together, let us fill homes all over the world with the most beautiful heart room, created by love to and from our children.

Can life be any bigger than that do you think?

About the illustrator

Meditation very often fosters creativity. Elsie Ralston has illustrated this book. She was born and raised in Peru. The love for her husband brought her to Denmark. Below you can see an image from the process of producing the illustrations for this book.

You can find Elsie on:
www.elsieralston.com

If you want more inspiration, keep an eye on:
www.gittewintergraugaard.dk

A Global Mission

Gitte Winter Graugaard is on a mission to help ONE MILLION CHILDREN and their families thrive through bedtime meditation. She is an expert in peaceful bedtime routines. She is a bestselling and award-winning author, and a TEDx speaker.

Her books are helping thousands of children to sleep in more than 20 countries. Gitte always reminds us to parent ourselves first before we parent our children and become aware of what we radiate.

To find more inspiration to conscious parenting and
better sleep, you can follow Gitte's blog on:

www.gittewintergraugaard.dk

To book Gitte for speaking or workshops go to:

www.gittewintergraugaard.com

Guidance and My Sleep Course

Having trouble getting your child to sleep?
You want some help? You're not alone. So many
parents around the world are struggling to help their
children to sleep. Find more help here:

www.inmyheart.eu

HEARTLIGHT

Teach your child to shine

This little book is a sequel to "In My Heart", a fifth meditation.
Here, your child learns to turn up their inner light in the
mountain of love and spread it around their whole body.
This meditation is also part of the book
"The Monster Manual for children who worry a lot".
Find out how to make your child a light bearer.

www.heartlight.eu

Meet Chief Eaglefeather
Meditations for children
BEDTIME STORIES
Let sleep come easily with these meditations.
Create a deep connection with your child and help them to recharge.
No 1
Gitte Winter Graugaard

The Flamedancers' Fire
Meditations for children
BEDTIME STORIES
Let sleep come easily with this FIRE meditation.
Create a deep connection with your child and help them to recharge.

Clear Cascade
Meditations for children
BEDTIME STORIES
Let sleep come easily with this WATER meditation.
Create a deep connection with your child and help them to recharge.
Gitte Winter Graugaard

The Deep Meadow
Meditations for children
BEDTIME STORIES
Let sleep come easily with this EARTH meditation.
Create a deep connection with your child and help them to recharge.
No 4
Gitte Winter Graugaard

The Mild Winds
Meditations for children
BEDTIME STORIES
Let sleep come easily with this AIR meditation.
Create a deep connection with your child and help them to recharge.
No 5
Gitte Winter Graugaard

All the books in the series The Valley of Hearts

In the first book you will learn how to arrive in the valley and you will meet your wise guide "Chief Eaglefeather".

As your child becomes more comfortable you can move further into the valley to encounter each of the elements. As you reach each new stage of the journey, new books and more meditations will be waiting for you.

"The Flamedancers' Fire" is book number two. You can benefit from using this meditation for children with lots of temper and conversely, for children with too little fire inside. Getting to know how to turn down or up your inner fire is crucial for how you cope in life.

"The Clear Cascade" in book number three is such a blessing to sensitive children and children prone to worry. It teaches us to cleanse our energy from other people before sleeping, which makes it a lot easier to feel our own energy and our own needs and boundaries.

Book number four is "The Deep Meadow", it is beneficial for all children in the Digital Age. Most children today need help to ground themselves.

We get to fly with "The Mild Winds" in book number five. The little daydreamers will love this meditation. However, it can also help children who need more perspective and creativity.

Each element has its own magical quality, which can be used to achieve peace of mind and to create better balance inside.

Please visit: www.thevalleyofhearts.com

Gitte is on a mission
to teach 1 MILLION children
to meditate. You can help her
by sharing this book and your
experiences with others. Ask for
her books at your local library,
or at your favourite bookshop and
use as presents to those you love.
Support her mission.

Thank you
for teaching
your child
to meditate.

See you soon ...